◩ READERS

Pre-level 1

Fishy Tales
Colorful Days
Garden Friends
Party Fun
In the Park
Farm Animals
Petting Zoo
Let's Make Music
Meet the Dinosaurs

Duck Pond Dip
My Dress-up Box
On the Move
Snakes Slither and Hiss
Family Vacation
Ponies and Horses
Cuentos de Peces *en español*
Dias Ilenos de color *en español*

Level 1

A Day at Greenhill Farm
Truck Trouble
Tale of a Tadpole
Surprise Puppy!
Duckling Days
A Day at Seagull Beach
Whatever the Weather
Busy Buzzy Bee
Big Machines
Wild Baby Animals
A Bed for the Winter
Born to be a Butterfly
Dinosaur's Day
Feeding Time
Diving Dolphin
Rockets and Spaceships
My Cat's Secret
First Day at Gymnastics
A Trip to the Zoo
I Can Swim!
A Trip to the Library
A Trip to the Doctor
A Trip to the Dentist
I Want To Be A Ballerina
Animal Hide and Seek

Submarines and Submersibles
Animals at Home
Let's Play Soccer
Homes Around the World
LEGO: Trouble at the Bridge
LEGO: Secret at Dolphin Bay
Star Wars: What is a Wookiee?
Star Wars: Ready, Set, Podrace!
Star Wars: Luke Skywalker's
    Amazing Story
Star Wars Clone Wars: Watch Out
    for Jabba the Hutt!
Power Rangers Jungle Fury: We are
    the Power Rangers
A Day in the Life of a Builder
A Day in the Life of a Dancer
A Day in the Life of a Firefighter
A Day in the Life of a Teacher
A Day in the Life of a Musician
A Day in the Life of a Doctor
A Day in the Life of a Police Officer
A Day in the Life of a TV Reporter
Gigantes de Hierro *en español*
Crías del mundo animal *en español*

A Note to Parents

DK READERS is a compelling program for beginning readers, designed in conjunction with leading literacy experts, including Dr. Linda Gambrell, Professor of Education at Clemson University. Dr. Gambrell has served as President of the International Reading Association, National Reading Conference, and College Reading Association.

Beautiful illustrations and superb full-color photographs combine with engaging, easy-to-read stories and informational texts to offer a fresh approach to each subject in the series. Each DK READER is guaranteed to capture a child's interest while developing his or her reading skills, general knowledge, and love of reading.

The five levels of DK READERS are aimed at different reading abilities, enabling you to choose the books that are exactly right for your child:

Pre-level 1: Learning to read

Level 1: Beginning to read

Level 2: Beginning to read alone

Level 3: Reading alone

Level 4: Proficient readers

The "normal" age at which a child begins to read can be anywhere from three to eight years old. Adult participation through the lower levels is very helpful for providing encouragement, discussing storylines, and sounding out unfamiliar words.

No matter which level you select, you can be sure that you are helping your child learn to read, then read to learn!

LONDON, NEW YORK,
MELBOURNE, MUNICH, and DELHI

Editor Victoria Taylor
Designer Owen Bennett
Senior Designer Lynne Moulding
Brand Manager Ron Stobbart
Art Director Lisa Lanzarini
Managing Editor Catherine Saunders
Publishing Manager Simon Beecroft
Category Publisher Alex Allan
Production Controller Clare McLean
Production Editor Siu Chan

Reading Consultant
Linda B. Gambrell, Ph.D.

First published in the United States in 2009
by DK Publishing
375 Hudson Street
New York, New York 10014

09 10 11 12 13 10 9 8 7 6 5 4 3 2 1
DD526—01/09

DK Books are available at special discounts when purchased in bulk
for sales promotions, premiums, fund-raising, or educational use.
For details, contact: DK Publishing Special Markets,
375 Hudson Street, New York, New York 10014
SpecialSales@dk.com

Published in Great Britain by Dorling Kindersley Limited.
A catalog record for this book is available from the Library of Congress.

ISBN: 978-0-7566-4510-6 (Paperback)
ISBN: 978-0-7566-4509-0 (Hardback)

Color reproduction by MDP
Printed and bound by L-Rex, China

Discover more at
www.dk.com
www.LEGO.com

 **READERS**

BEGINNING **1** TO READ

On the Farm

Written by Victoria Taylor

This is a farmer.

He sometimes drives a
tractor around the farm.

There are many
animals on the farm.
Come and meet them!

This is a cow.
Cows go 'moo'.

'Baa' says the sheep
on the hill.

This is a horse.
Horses go 'naay'.

This is a pig.
Pigs go 'oink'.

'Woof-woof' says
the farmer's dog.

This is a cat.
Cats go 'meow'.

'Cock-a-doodle-do'.
The hen wakes
everyone up.

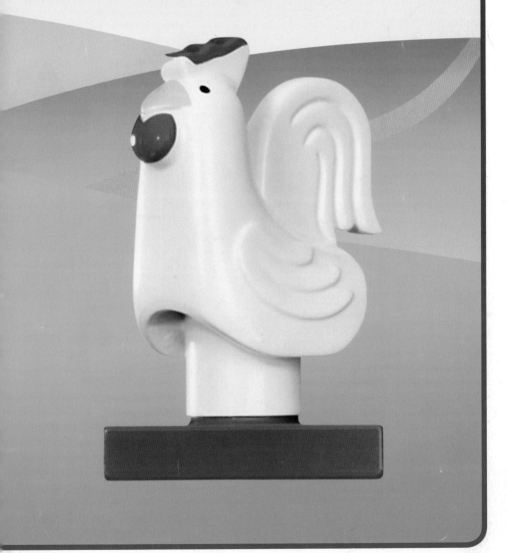

Sometimes the farmer's children ride the horses. It's great fun!

The horses also have a
cart that the children
can ride in.

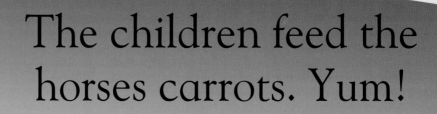

The children feed the
horses carrots. Yum!

The horses can jump
over fences.
They have won a
trophy for jumping!

The farmer's family has a pet dog. He has spots on his coat.

They also have a pet
cat. The cat likes to sit
near the horses' stable.

There is a baby pig on
the farm. Baby pigs are
called piglets.

This piglet sometimes sits in the farmer's wheelbarrow.

This is the farm's helper.

He drives the combine
harvester. A combine
harvester is a machine
that cuts corn.

Combine harvesters
make hay bales and
drop them out of the
back of the machine.

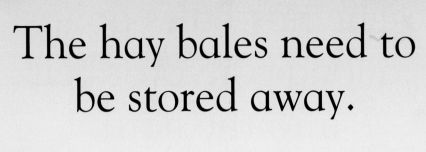

The hay bales need to
be stored away.

The hay bales go up a long conveyor belt into the barn.

The farmer's wife helps to store them away.

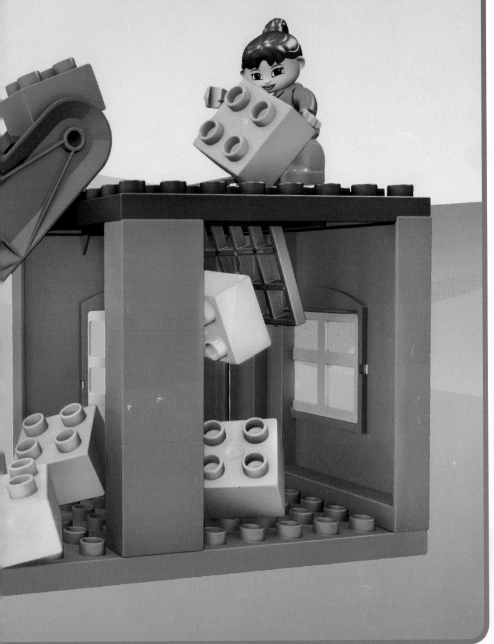

The tractor can pull
a plow. The plow turns
soil over so it will be
ready for planting.

A roller can be fixed to the tractor. The roller flattens the soil so seeds can be planted.

There is always a lot to do on the farm.

Even the farm animals
sometimes need a rest!

Picture Word List

Sheep

Piglet

Harvester

Cow

Horse

Tractor

DK READERS

My name is

_____

I have read this book

Date